Managing Our Resources

Water
A resource our world depends on

Heinemann Library
Chicago, Illinois

Ian Graham

© 2005 Heinemann Library

a division of Capstone Global Library, LLC.

Chicago, Illinois

Customer Service 888-454-2279

Visit our website at www.heinemannlibrary.
com

Designed by David Poole and
Paul Myerscough
Photo research by Melissa Allison and
Andrea Sadler

Originated by Ambassador Litho Ltd.
Printed and bound in the United States of
America in North Mankato, Minnesota.
112012   007051

14 13 12

10 9 8 7 6 5 4 3 2

**Library of Congress Cataloging-in-
Publication Data**
Graham, Ian, 1953-
  Water : a resource our world depends on /
Ian Graham.
      p. cm. -- (Managing our resources)
  Includes bibliographical references and
index.
  ISBN 1-4034-5620-8 (hc : lib. bdg.) --
  ISBN 1-4034-5628-3 (pb)
  1. Water--Juvenile literature. I. Title. II.
Series.
  GB662.3.G72 2005
  553.7--dc22
                                    2004005910

Acknowledgments
The author and publisher are grateful to the
following for permission to reproduce
copyright material: p. 4 Adam Woolfitt/
Corbis; pp. 5 top, 5 bottom, 12,
15, 22 Photodisc/Getty Images; p. 6 Roy
Morsch/Corbis; p. 7 bottom Jim Richardson/
Corbis; p. 7 top Vince Streano/Corbis; p. 8
Hubert Stadler/Corbis; p. 9 NASA; p. 10
Norbert Schaefer/Corbis;
p. 11 Peter Johnson/Corbis; p. 13 Fraser
Hall/Robert Harding Picture Library; p. 14
Paul Seheult/Corbis; p. 16 Jeff Edwards/
Harcourt Education Ltd.; pp. 17 top, 19 top,
27 ImageWorks/Topham Picturepoint; pp. 17
bottom, 18 Stuart P. Donachie/Ecoscene/
Corbis; p. 19 bottom Photri/Topham
Picturepoint; p. 20 Kontas Yannis/Sygma/
Corbis; p. 21 top Bryn Colton/Assignment
Photographers/ Corbis; p. 21 bottom Najlah
Feanny/SABA/Corbis; p. 23 Graham Neden/
Ecoscene; p. 24 left David Warren/FLPA; p.
24 right Sally Morgan/Ecoscene/ Corbis; p.
25 S. Jonasson/FLPA; p. 26 Yann Arthus-
Bertrand/Corbis; p. 28 top Philip Gould/
Corbis; p. 29 James Field/Simon Girling
Associates/Harcourt Education Ltd.

Cover photograph: Corbis.

Contents

Some words are shown in bold, **like this.** You can find
out what they mean by looking in the glossary.

What Is Water?

Water is a natural resource. It is usually found in liquid form, but it can also be a solid or a gas. At room temperature, water is a clear liquid. Pure water has no taste or smell.

Water is made from two simpler substances called **hydrogen** and oxygen that are joined together. Each **molecule** of water contains one **atom** of oxygen linked to two atoms of hydrogen. The chemical formula of water is H_2O.

Water exists in three different forms in nature—liquid (water), solid (ice or snow), and gas (water vapor).

When is water liquid, solid, or gas?

The state of water—solid, liquid, or gas—depends on the temperature of water. If the temperature falls to 32 °F (0 °C), water turns to ice. If water is heated to 212 °F (100 °C), it will boil and become a gas. When water changes into a gas, the gas is called steam or water **vapor**. When steam cools down, it changes back into water again.

Why does ice float?

Ice floats on water because water behaves differently than most substances. Most liquid substances shrink as they cool down and become solid. These solid pieces are heavier than the liquid and so they sink. Water is different. Just before it freezes, it expands and becomes lighter, so it floats.If water inside a pipe freezes,it can burst the pipe.

When warm, moist air touches something cold, such as a chilled glass, some of the moisture cools down and changes into water droplets on the glass. This is also why a mirror mists over when you breathe on it.

Ice cubes float on top of a glass of water because they are lighter than the liquid water.

What Is Water Used For?

Water is used for many things, including cooking, washing, heating, and cooling. It also provides the power that makes some machines work.

Why is water used for washing?

Water is good for washing because it carries dirt away. It also dissolves, or breaks down, some substances. Water and grease do not mix, but hot water can melt grease and it can be washed away. Soapy water removes greasy stains even better because soap surrounds **particles** of grease and keeps them in the water.

How is water used for heating?

Many homes and workplaces are warmed by water. The water is heated in a tank called a boiler and then pumped through pipes to **radiators.** When each radiator fills up with hot water, it heats everything near it. The water then returns to the boiler and is reheated.

One important use for water is cooking.

How does water cool things?

If something hot is dipped in cold water, the heat flows out of it into the water. Blacksmiths cool hot metals by dipping them in water. You use water to keep your body cool, too. When you feel hot, glands in your skin produce sweat, which is mostly water. Heat from your body makes the sweat **evaporate,** leaving you feeling cooler.

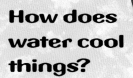

Firefighters use water to put out fires.

How is water used to grow crops?

Plants, including crops that provide the food we eat, need water to grow. Large areas of land are too dry to grow crops. Extra water is sometimes brought in through pipelines. Providing extra water for farmland in this manner is called irrigation.

Irrigation is needed to grow some crops in dry parts of the world.

How does water help us do work?

Moving water has energy, so it can make other things move, too. If a wheel is dipped into flowing water, the water turns it. Adding paddles to the wheel makes the wheel turn faster. A wheel with paddles used in water is called a waterwheel. People have used waterwheels for about 3,000 years. They were mainly used to turn millstones that ground corn into flour for making bread.

Today, we use water to make electricity. Engineers use water rushing through a pipe to spin a **turbine**. The turbine drives a generator, a machine that makes electricity. Also, when water is heated to 212 °F (100 °C), it changes to steam. Steam takes up much more space than water. It pushes out in all directions. The force of the steam can be used to spin a turbine or power a generator.

Did you know?

One way to make salt is to use the Sun's heat to dry out shallow pans of saltwater. When the water **evaporates**, it leaves behind the salt.

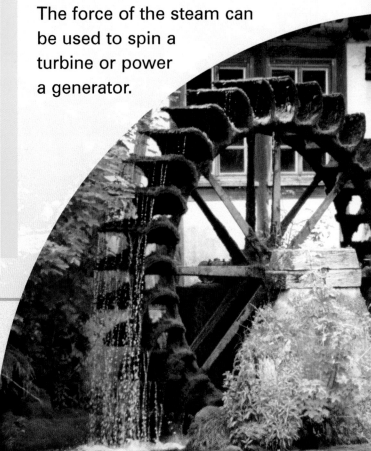

Waterwheels, like this one in Germany, have been used to power mills for centuries.

CASE STUDY:
The Space Shuttle Space Suit

It is very hard for an astronaut wearing a space suit to keep cool. When an astronaut gets hot and sweats, the sweat is trapped inside the suit. The sweat cannot carry heat away from the astronaut's body. Astronauts keep cool in a different way.

Inside their space suits, astronauts wear tight-fitting vests and pants with 330 feet (100 meters) of plastic tubes sewn into them. Water is pumped through the tubes. The cool water is warmed by the astronaut's body and carries the heat away. The water is then cooled down inside the suit's backpack and pumped around the astronaut's body again. The astronaut can adjust the temperature of the water to keep his or her body comfortable.

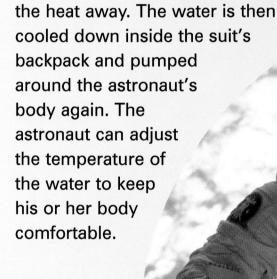

Astronauts wear a special suit that uses water to keep them from getting too hot.

Why Is Water Important for Life?

Water is necessary for life to exist. Life on Earth probably began in the sea. Millions of years later, some sea creatures crawled onto the land. They developed into new creatures, including dinosaurs. After millions more years, human beings developed. Although humans live on land, water is still very important. More than half the weight of the human body is water.

How much water do we need?

Every day people need to drink about 68 ounces (2 liters) of water, or about 8 glasses. You need more on a hot day or if you are exercising. You lose water by sweating and even when you breathe. Did you know that the lining of your lungs is moist? Every time you breathe out, some of the moisture is carried out with the air. All of this water has to be replaced. You get some water from drinks and some from food.

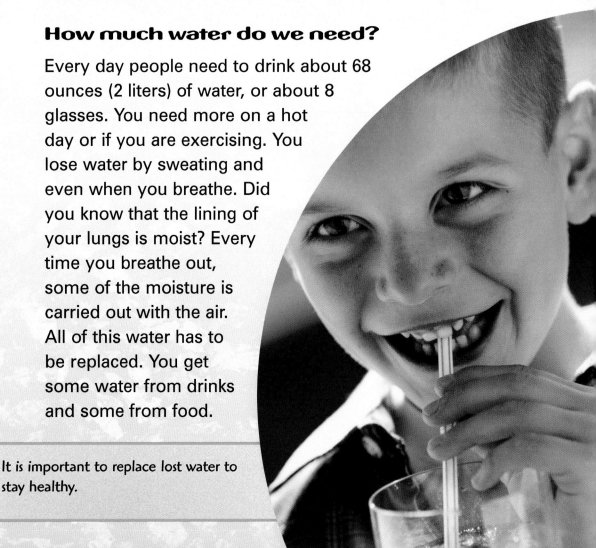

It is important to replace lost water to stay healthy.

How do living things use water?

Most plants and animals are made from tiny cells that contain water. The water fills the cells and helps them keep their shape. If a plant is not watered enough, some of the plant cells become limp and the plant wilts. Water also carries food and other substances around inside plants and animals to help their cells work properly.

Some animals can store extra water inside their bodies. Some people think camels store water in their humps. Actually, a camel's hump contains fat, which the camel lives on when food is scarce. Camels store water in their blood. A camel can drink almost 25 gallons (100 liters) of water at a time.

It is difficult for plants and animals to survive in places where there is little water.

Where Is Water Found?

Water is found nearly everywhere on Earth. Almost three quarters of Earth's surface is covered with water. Almost all of it is seawater, which contains salt. Rivers, lakes, **glaciers,** and the **polar ice caps** contain freshwater, which does not contain salt. Water is also found all over Earth as rain. Rain is considered freshwater.

Where does all the rain go?

Some rain runs off the land into rivers and lakes. This is called surface water. Some rain sinks into the land and collects underground. Water that collects underground is called groundwater. Rock with lots of tiny holes in it soaks up the water like a sponge. These water-filled rocks are called **aquifers.**

Earth looks blue from space because of all the water in its oceans and **atmosphere.**

Did you know?

Earth is the only planet known to have liquid water on its surface.

CASE STUDY:
Lake Mead

Lake Mead is the biggest **reservoir** in the United States. Lake Mead is 115 miles (185 kilometers) long and up to 10 miles (16 kilometers) wide. It was created in the 1930s when the Hoover Dam was built across the Colorado River on the Arizona–Nevada border. As the water was blocked behind the dam, it formed Lake Mead.

Lake Mead not only supplies drinking water—it is also used to make electricity. Huge pipes carry water inside the dam, where it drives the generators that make the electricity. Enough water rushes through the generators to fill fifteen swimming pools every second. The electricity generated supplies 500,000 homes.

The Hoover Dam, a 725-foot- (221-meter-) high concrete wall, holds back the waters of the Colorado River to form Lake Mead.

How Is Water Processed?

We can do many things to water. It can be **processed** in many different ways. One of the simplest ways is to heat it. Water is heated for cooking food and making drinks such as tea and coffee. Boiling water kills any germs it may contain. Also, as we have seen, hot water can be used to carry energy from one place to another by pumping the water through pipes.

Another way to use water is to mix substances with it or dissolve substances in it. Watercolor paints are made by mixing colored materials, called pigments, with water. Sugar is often dissolved in drinks to make them taste sweeter.

This water was heated until it started to boil. Pure water boils at a temperature of 212 °F (100 °C).

How is water processed to make it safe?

Water is made safe to drink at water treatment plants. First, the tiny **particles** of mud and plants that make water cloudy are removed. This is done by adding chemicals that make the particles stick together, so that they sink. Smaller particles are removed by sending air bubbles through the water. The bubbles carry the particles to the surface, where they are skimmed off. Any remaining particles are taken out by letting the water flow through sand, which traps the particles. Any living **organisms** in the water are killed by a disinfectant, such as chlorine. In some countries, fluoride is also added to tap water to reduce tooth decay.

Water in swimming pools has chlorine added to it to make it safe for people to swim in.

Did you know?

Travelers and climbers in wild places sometimes have to drink water straight from rivers or lakes. They can make the water safe to drink by adding **iodine** tablets to it or boiling it to kill harmful organisms.

How Does Nature Move Water Around?

The Sun's warmth **evaporates** water from the oceans, forming water **vapor**. The vapor rises until it reaches cold air high above the ground, where it changes back into water droplets. The droplets form clouds in the sky. The water then falls back to Earth as rain or snow. The water runs down over the land and back into the oceans. This continuous movement of water in nature is called the water cycle.

When water evaporates from the oceans, most of it stays in the air for about ten days before it falls back to Earth. Water that falls into the oceans stays there for much longer before it evaporates again—about 37,000 years!

Water is constantly moving from the surface of Earth into the **atmosphere** and back again.

The water cycle

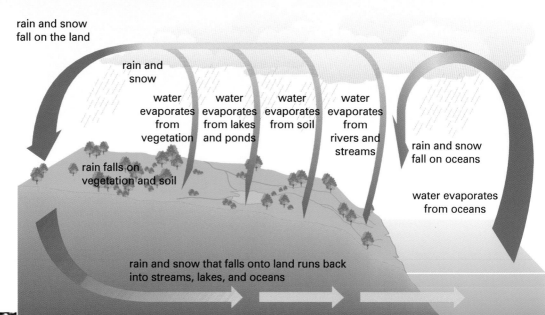

rain and snow fall on the land

rain and snow

water evaporates from vegetation

water evaporates from lakes and ponds

water evaporates from soil

water evaporates from rivers and streams

rain and snow fall on oceans

rain falls on vegetation and soil

water evaporates from oceans

rain and snow that falls onto land runs back into streams, lakes, and oceans

How do plants move water?

Plants move a huge amount of water from the land to the air. They take up water from the ground through their roots. It escapes into the air as water vapor through tiny holes in their leaves.

How do the oceans move water?

Water flows through the oceans in currents, like rivers flowing through the sea. Near Earth's poles, water cools down. Cold water is heavier than warm water, so it sinks. It flows toward the equator, where it rises and warms before flowing back to the poles. This journey takes about 1,000 years.

Water flows downhill from mountains and hills to the sea.

Did you know?

Scientists have used toy ducks to study ocean currents. In 1992 thousands of rubber ducks fell off a ship in the Pacific Ocean. Currents carried them north. They were trapped in ice for five years, slowly drifting around Canada. They reached the Atlantic Ocean in the year 2000. Some were carried toward Europe while others drifted toward the United States.

How Do People Transport Water?

Water is so essential for life that it has always been transported from where it occurs in nature to wherever people live. In the ancient world, it was collected from rivers, lakes, and wells in buckets, barrels, jars, and bags.

Traditional methods of lifting water from rivers are still used today.

When people started living in towns and cities, they had to bring water in to meet their needs. They did it by building channels to carry water from nearby rivers and lakes. These artificial waterways were called aqueducts. About 2,000 years ago, 11 aqueducts brought 42 million gallons (189 million liters) of water into the city of Rome, Italy, every day. It flowed into buildings through pipes made from lead.

Today, cities can be built almost anywhere because water can be supplied by pipelines. Some cities in the United States have been built in deserts. One of these is Las Vegas, Nevada. Most of its water is piped in from Lake Mead. Some of the city's water comes from an **aquifer.**

How is water transported today?

Today water is transported in many different ways. It is supplied to homes and businesses by pumping it through underground pipes. The pipes keep clean drinking water separate from dirty groundwater and wastewater, or sewage. Burying water pipes also stops the water from freezing in winter. In places where the water supply has broken down, water can be delivered to people in **tanker** trucks.

Fire trucks carry enough water in their tanks to deal with small fires, but they can also pump water up from underground water pipes or nearby rivers.

Water gets to your home through pipes buried under the ground.

Did you know?

People all over the world drink about 24 billion gallons (89 billion liters) of bottled water a year. About 3.4 billion gallons (13 billion liters) are drunk in the United States alone.

CASE STUDY:
Firefighting Aircraft

The Bombardier 415 is a firefighting aircraft. It has big tanks inside it to hold water. It is designed so that the tanks can be filled quickly and then used to drop the water onto a fire to help put it out.

The plane's tanks can hold more than 1,585 gallons (6,000 liters) of water. It can fill its tanks in only 12 seconds by scooping up water from a lake or the sea while it skims across the surface, still flying. Then, as it flies over a fire, it can drop all the water in less than 1 second.

Firefighting planes are used in countries such as Canada, which have large forests and also many lakes. If there is a forest fire, the planes can fill up their tanks at a nearby lake and then empty their tanks on the fire.

Firefighting planes are designed to carry water instead of passengers.

How Can Water Affect the Way We Live?

Water has the power to affect our lives in good and bad ways. Storms, rain, and high tides can cause floods. Serious floods can destroy homes and crops. The sea can eat away at the coast so much that cliffs collapse and buildings fall into the sea. Sometimes water contains high levels of bacteria, or **organisms** that can cause disease.

Beach houses and other buildings sometimes slide down cliffs as a result of waves eroding the coast.

How does water change the land?

Tides coming in and going out and the constant pounding of waves on the land washes the ground away in some places. This is called coastal erosion.

The state of Missouri suffered serious flooding in 2000. A series of thunderstorms dropped more than 14 inches (35 centimeters) of rain in only 6 hours.

Storm surges

Big storms sometimes suck the sea upward, like water being sucked up a straw. Strong winds can then blow the water against a coast. This is called a storm surge. In 1953 a storm surge in the North Sea raised the sea level by up to 13 feet (4 meters). Floods along the coasts of the United Kingdom and the Netherlands killed more than 2,300 people.

Hurricanes are very powerful storms that can create large storm surges. One of the worst hurricanes to hit the United States was Hurricane Andrew in 1992. It produced a storm surge of more than sixteen feet (five meters) near Florida.

Earthquakes at sea

Earthquakes sometimes happen underneath the sea. When the seabed moves, it can make waves called tsunamis. These are small when they are far out at sea, but they can cross an ocean at the speed of a jet. In shallow water near land, they slow down and pile up higher.

Earthquakes under the sea can cause powerful waves that flood low-lying land.

Did you know?

Tsunami is a Japanese word meaning "harbor wave." Tsunamis can cause horrible damage to harbors.

Tsunamis can grow from less than 3 feet (1 meter) high at sea to 100 feet (30 meters) high near land. When a tsunami hits a coast, it sweeps away everything in front of it.

How might the sea change in future?

If the sea level all over the world were to change, the results could be disastrous. Many scientists believe that Earth is getting warmer. If this causes the **polar ice caps** at Earth's north and south poles to melt, the extra water would make the sea deeper everywhere. Towns and cities near coasts would be flooded. Some islands could disappear altogether. The islands of Tuvalu in the Pacific Ocean are, at most, only 13 feet (4 meters) above sea level. They are already suffering from rising sea levels and could disappear altogether within 50 years.

Huge chunks of ice have been breaking off the polar ice caps at Earth's poles and melting. Antarctica's Larsen B ice shelf, which contained about 500 billion tons of ice, started breaking up and collapsed in 2002.

CASE STUDY:
The Thames River Barrier, London

London has been flooded several times by water flowing in from the North Sea up the Thames River, which runs through the city. Today London is protected from flooding by a barrier. Nine concrete islands, called piers, stand in a line across the river. There are steel gates between the piers. The gates are very strong and heavy. The four longest gates weigh more than 1,500 tons each. They usually lie flat on the riverbed so that ships can pass through. If there is any risk of flooding, machines inside the piers swing the gates upright to close off the river and keep the rising waters out of the city.

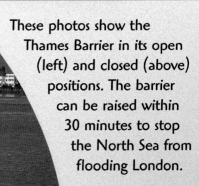

These photos show the Thames Barrier in its open (left) and closed (above) positions. The barrier can be raised within 30 minutes to stop the North Sea from flooding London.

Why Should We Protect Water?

Water is necessary for life, so we need to make sure that we have enough clean water that is safe to drink. We also have to make sure that rivers, lakes, and the sea remain clean enough for fish and other water creatures to live in because they are an important source of food.

Is there enough water for everyone?

It may seem as though there is more than enough water for everyone because most of Earth is covered with water. However, most plants and animals on land depend on freshwater to survive. Only a tiny amount of the water on Earth is freshwater, and most of that is frozen at the north and south poles.

The sea is an important source of food, so we must look after the oceans and keep them clean.

People in poor countries often find it difficult to get enough clean freshwater. Even when there is enough water, it may be dangerous to drink. Poisoning is a serious problem in the country of Bangladesh because water in some wells contains a poison called arsenic. It comes from the rock that the water trickles through on its way to the wells.

Developed countries can afford to provide their people with clean drinking water, but even these countries cannot provide more water than nature supplies. For example, the state of California is running out of freshwater. One reason for this is because the state's population grew from 16 million in the 1960s to 35 million today. The state plans to make the extra freshwater it needs by taking the salt out of seawater. This is called desalting or desalination.

Seawater can be changed into fresh drinking water by taking the salt out of it. This desalination plant is in Kuwait.

How Can We Protect Water?

We can protect and conserve water in a number of ways. We can try not to waste it by taking as little as possible from nature. We can also try to stop water from becoming **polluted** with harmful substances such as oil and chemicals.

How can we use less water?

We use more water than we need to. We can use less water at home by only using washing machines and dishwashers when they are full. We could take a lot less water from nature by repairing leaks in underground water pipes. In some places, more than half of the water sent out does not reach people because of leaks.

One easy way to save water is to turn off the faucet while you brush your teeth.

How can we reduce pollution?

Pollution is reduced by cleaning dirty water from homes and businesses before it is released into rivers and the sea. Waste water treatment plants do this important job. Gardeners and farmers can help by reducing the amounts of chemicals that they spray on the land so that fewer chemicals are washed into rivers by rain. It is also important to reduce pollution in the air because air pollution mixes with moisture in the air and enters the water cycle in rain.

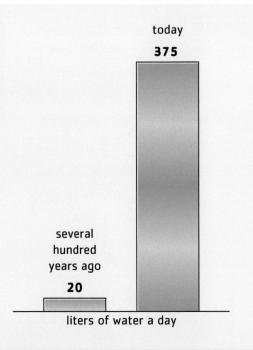

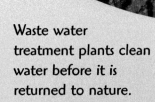

Waste water treatment plants clean water before it is returned to nature.

Did you know?

If you lived a few hundred years ago, you would probably use less than 5 gallons (20 liters) of water a day for all of your needs. We use a lot more water today. It is used for heating and in washing machines and dishwashers. People also wash themselves more often today than they did long ago. The average American uses up to 100 gallons (375 liters) of water every day.

today
375

several
hundred
years ago
20

liters of water a day

Will Water Ever Run Out?

Water will not run out because it is never completely used up. It is constantly being **recycled** by nature. Drops of rain falling on us today might once have been drunk by a dinosaur. The water we use goes back into nature and it will be used again and again for millions of years to come.

However, we must continue to protect and conserve water. Plants and animals can only use clean water. Many rivers and lakes that were once badly polluted are now much cleaner. In many countries, governments have passed laws to stop people and factories from polluting bodies of water.

Did you know?
In 1858 the Thames River, which flows through London, was so polluted that it smelled horrible. The smell forced British government leaders to approve a plan to build a new sewage system. Today the Thames River is known as one of the world's cleanest rivers. Fish and even seals live in the river.

The same water has been part of Earth's water cycle for hundreds of millions of years.

Glossary

aquifer layer of rock, sand, or gravel that is able to hold water

atmosphere mixture of gases that surrounds a planet or a moon in space

atom smallest particle of an element

evaporate change from a liquid state into a vapor

glacier body of ice that slowly moves down a valley or slope or across a land surface

hydrogen chemical element that is found in nature as a flammable, colorless, and odorless gas

iodine nonmetallic element that can be used in combination with alcohol to kill germs

molecule smallest particle of a substance having all the properties of that substance

organism living plant or animal

particle very small bit of something

polar ice cap large covering of ice, such as those present at Earth's north and south poles

pollution harmful or poisonous substances in nature, usually produced by the activities of humans

process to change a material by a series of actions or treatments or the method by which a material is changed

radiator device with hot water flowing through it, designed to heat a room

recycle to process for reuse instead of using materials only once and then throwing them away

reservoir place where something, such as water, is kept for use in the future

tanker vehicle or ship designed to carry a large amount of liquid

turbine engine with winglike parts that are spun around by the pressure of water, steam, or gas

vapor fine particles of matter that float in and cloud the air

More Books to Read

Bailey, Jacqui. *A Drop in the Ocean: The Story of Water.* Minneapolis, Minn.: Picture Window Books, 2004.

Ballard, Carol. *Water.* Chicago: Raintree, 2004.

Dalgleish, Sharon. *Saving Water.* Broomall, Pa.: Chelsea House Publishers, 2003.

Donald, Rhonda Lucas. *Water Pollution.* Danbury, Conn.: Scholastic Library, 2002.

Murphy, Brian. *Water.* Chanhassen, Minn.: Creative Publishing, 2004.

Trueit, Trudi Strain. *The Water Cycle.* Danbury, Conn.: Scholastic Library, 2002.

Parker, Steve. *Water Power.* Milwaukee, Wis.: Gareth Stevens, 2004.

Spilsbury, Louise, and Richard Spilsbury. *Sweeping Tsunamis.* Chicago, Heinemann Library, 2003.

Index